Chosen In Eternity

OTHER BOOKS
BY
JOHN G. REISINGER

Abraham's Four Seeds
But I Say Unto You
Christ, Lord and Lawgiver Over the Church
Grace
Our Sovereign God
Tablets of Stone
The Sovereignty of God in Prayer
The Sovereignty of God in Providence
What is the Christian Faith?

Chosen In Eternity

John G. Reisinger

NEW COVENANT MEDIA

5317 Wye Creek Drive, Frederick, MD 21703-6938

Phone: 301-473-8781 or 800-376-4146   Fax: 301-473-5128
Website: www.soundofgracebooks.com
Email: info@soundofgracebooks.com

In this book, the author has placed certain words from Scriptural quotations in italics or bold print without individually marking each instance with such words as "italics mine." The reader should be aware, however, that these italics and bold print are not found in the original texts but are added by the author for reasons of emphasis and clarity.

Chosen In Eternity
Copyright © 2000 by John G. Reisinger
ISBN 1-928965-04-0
Requests for information should be addressed to:
New Covenant Media
5317 Wye Creek Drive
Frederick, MD 21703-6938

Scripture quotations marked (NIV) are taken from the HOLY BIBLE, NEW INTERNATIONAL VERSION® NIV® Copyright©1973, 1978, 1984 by International Bible Society. Used by permission. All rights reserved.

All other Scripture quotations are taken from the King James Version.

All rights reserved. No part of this publication may be reproduced, stored in a retrieval system, or transmitted in any form or by any means—electronic, mechanical, photocopy, recording, or any other—except for brief quotations in printed reviews, without the prior permission of the publisher.

Writers and speakers often use the words *predestination* and *election* interchangeably. However, this usage may create confusion. Predestination is the truth that God sovereignly purposes everything that will ever happen. He sovereignly brings to pass everything that he himself has planned (cf. Rom. 11:36, NIV). This includes every event of every person's life, and everything about that person, down to the very hairs of their heads (cf. Matt. 10:30, NIV). The many verses that speak of "all things" being under God's sovereign control can only be true if predestination is true (cf. Rom. 8:28, NIV). Election is the truth of predestination applied to one specific area, or one category of the "all" things, namely, our personal salvation. The doctrine of election is the truth that God sovereignly chooses, or elects, certain individuals to be saved.

You have probably heard the following popular illustration about election. This is what I was taught in Bible School.

> I believe in election because the Bible teaches election. However, it is a true *election* in that it involves voting. First, God votes for you. Then, the Devil votes against you. And lastly, you cast the deciding vote. Now that is a wonderful illustration but it is the worst theology possible. Someone has noted that (1) this makes God and the Devil equal in power. The Devil has the power to deadlock God and frustrate His purposes; (2) man is mightier than both God and the Devil because he alone has the power to break the deadlock. Someone else has said, 'In this election the Devil was not a registered voter and since you were of non-age you were not able to vote. That leaves only one vote—God's!

I want to emphasize at the very beginning of this booklet that not all sincere Christians agree with my understanding of the subject of election. If you have never heard this subject discussed or taught, it may "throw you for a loop" the first time you hear it. I urge you not to believe it just because someone else does; and likewise, do not reject it because your favorite preacher does not believe it. Prove that you have a Berean spirit and look at the texts of Scripture and see what they are actually saying. If you disagree with my understanding of election, that does not mean you do not love God. I have personal friends who love the Savior just as much as I do and disagree with me about election. John Calvin will not be at heaven's gate interviewing you about your view of election. You may be wrong about many subjects and still go to heaven, but you cannot be wrong about trusting the Lord Jesus Christ as your Lord and Savior. However, the Bible does say a lot about "God choosing some sinners" and we must understand in some way the many verses that use these words.

The Bible teaches something about both *predestination* and *election*.

The words *predestination, election, chosen, foreordained,* and *called* are used many times in the Bible. Whether we like it or not, we not only *must believe something* about this subject, but we must also realize that everyone *else believes* something about election. "I don't believe in predestination" does not mean, "I do not believe the words *predestination* or *election* are in the Bible," since everyone knows those words are in the Bible. No, "I do not believe in predestination" really means, "I do not believe the Bible means *what you are saying it does* when it talks about predestination." In other words, you must deny the very Word of God to reject predestination and election outright, but you are not necessarily denying the Bible just because you disagree with my interpretation. You cannot deny that Jesus said, "Ye have not chosen me, but I have chosen you," (John 15:16a) or you are denying the Word of God. You may, however, disagree with what I think those words mean without rejecting the Bible. You will, of course, be wrong in your understanding of election, but like me, you have been wrong before. Seriously, I repeat: sincere and godly Christians can, and do, disagree about what Jesus and the Apostles meant when they talked about election.

Those familiar with the Doctrines of Grace will recognize that in this booklet we are dealing with the second point of those five doctrines. We are discussing what is called "Unconditional Election."

Unconditional Election, or Grace *purposed,* deals with the work of God the Father in the scheme of redemption. All agree that God "chooses some people to be saved," but they differ greatly about *why* he chooses one and not another. The religion of free will says, "Yes, God chose some sinners to be saved just as he sovereignly chose Israel. However, he chose Christians purely on the basis of his foreknowledge." By foreknowledge, these people mean that before time began, God looked down through history and "foresaw" beforehand who would be "willing" to accept Christ, and on the basis of this "foreseen faith" in some people, God chose these particular people to be saved. It only takes a moment's reflection to realize that in such a scheme, God has not actually done any choosing at all. All God has done is ratify the sinner's pre-known choice. What else can that idea mean?

It is to counter this wrong idea that we add the word *unconditional* to the word *election*. We mean to emphasize that God's election of some sinner is totally unconditioned by anything known or foreseen in the sinner. Election is based solely on the unconditioned sovereign choice of God. If God *foresaw* what the sinner, with his free will, was going to do (namely, choose to be saved) and God then decided to "choose," based entirely on the foreknown information about that particular sinner, how can God be said to have chosen in any sense whatever? That sound like double talk to me. The most that could be said was that God is merely agreeing with what he foresaw was going to happen and decided to ratify the sinner's choice. Thus, God looked into the future and foresaw I would be different from other people because I would be willing to believe the gospel. God's reaction to my foreknown decision was, "Great! I foresee your willingness and that gives me a basis or foundation upon which I can choose you to be saved." If you believe that, please do not say that God, in any sense whatsoever, chooses in salvation. Be honest and say, "The one reason God was able to choose me to be saved was the fact that he foresaw that I would choose him first. He foresaw that I was not stupid like those who reject the gospel. God saw that I had a better heart, one that was willing to give him a chance to save me." I'm sure many will object and say, "But I never said that." Maybe you did not say that out loud but that is exactly what your view of foreknowledge is saying.

On the other hand, the religion of free grace insists that apart from God first giving faith as a gift, no sinner would ever have any faith to be foreseen. God *sovereignly* chooses "whom he will" (cf. Rom. 9:10–13; 18–25) and his choice is totally "unconditioned" by anything foreseen in the creature. So the real question is not "Does God choose some sinners to be saved," but rather, is his choice "conditioned" by the foreseen willingness of the sinner or is God's choice totally "unconditional," or sovereign, based solely on his own good pleasure?

There are four basic questions that must be asked in any discussion of election. We will seek to answer these questions with specific texts of Scripture.

(1) Who does the electing—God or man? The biblical answer is "God." "Ye have not chosen me, but I have chosen you..." John 15:16a

(2) When did the electing, or choosing, take place—in eternity or in time? The biblical answer is "in eternity." "Who hath saved us, and

called us with an holy calling, not according to our works, but according to his own purpose and grace, which was given us in Christ Jesus *before the world began*..." 2 Tim 1:9

(3) On what basis was the electing, or choosing, done: Was it based on free grace (*i.e.,* unconditional) or was it based on man's choice (*i.e.,* conditioned by, free will)? "Even so then at this present time also there is a remnant according to the election of grace. And if by grace, then is it no more of works: otherwise grace is no more grace. But if it be of works, then is it no more grace: otherwise work is no more work" (Rom 11:5–6).

(4) Does this election involve personal salvation or only privileges and service? "But we are bound to give thanks alway to God for you, brethren beloved of the Lord, because God hath from the beginning *chosen you to salvation* through sanctification of the Spirit and belief of the truth..." 2 Thess. 2:13

The Biblical meaning of *chose*

Perhaps it would be well to fix in our minds how the Bible uses the word *chose*. Exactly what does God want us to understand when he says that he "chose us in Christ"? Look at the following text and ask yourself, "Exactly what did David do in this situation?"

> And he [David] took his staff in his hand, and *chose* him five smooth stones out of the brook, and put them in a shepherd's bag which he had, even in a scrip; and his sling was in his hand: and he drew near to the Philistine" (1 Sam 17:40).

What ever *chose* means in reference to those five stones, it means exactly the same thing that God did in reference to everyone whom he "chooses to be saved." Can anyone believe that those five stones somehow, possibly by wiggling a bit, indicated to David that they were *willing* to be chosen? No, everyone will see David sovereignly deciding which stones best suited his purpose. No one will dispute that the choice of the particular stones was totally in David's mind and purpose and not in the willingness of the stones. That is precisely what it means when the Scriptures say, "God *chose* us!" Just as David deliberately chose those five specific stones, and just as God chose one particular nation, Israel, out of all the other nations, so God deliberately chose specific individuals to be saved by his grace. Some may say, "Yes, but we are not lifeless stones." That may be true, but we were just as spiritually lifeless and dead as those stones were lifeless and dead. Our hearts were just as hard and cold as those stones, but the grace and power of God took out those stony hearts and gave us a heart of flesh (cf. Ezek. 36:26).

Election in the Old Testament Scriptures

The nation of Israel is a classic proof of the doctrine of sovereign election. Deuteronomy 7:6–8 is a typical passage that describes Israel's unique relationship with God and how that relationship came about.

> For thou art an holy people unto the LORD thy God: the LORD thy God hath chosen thee to be a special people unto himself, above all people that are upon the face of the earth. The LORD did not set his love upon you, nor choose you, because ye were more in number than any people; for ye were the fewest of all people: But because the LORD loved you, and because he would keep the oath which he had sworn unto your fathers, hath the LORD brought you out with a mighty hand, and redeemed you out of the house of bondmen, from the hand of Pharaoh king of Egypt (Deut. 7:6–8).

Everyone agrees that Israel was "the *chosen* nation" of God. The question is *not*, "Did God sovereignly choose the nation of Israel out from among all of the other nations to be his special property?" You would have to literally deny the Bible before you could reject that clear truth. The only question is, "*Why* did he choose *that particular* nation as his special people?" And the only two answers you can give are either, (1) because God foresaw they were 'willing' to be chosen, or (2) because God sovereignly chose them simply because he wanted to choose them. What does the above Scripture say? Jacob's children were chosen because of the sovereign oath that God made to their father Abraham long before they were born. That choice had absolutely nothing to do with Israel's willingness. It is so with us who believe. We are saved by an oath the Father made to his Son long before we were born and that oath has nothing to do with our so-called "free will."

Election is clearly taught in the New Testament Scriptures

Our Lord Jesus taught the doctrine of election. We will confine our references to the Gospel of John since that book is known as the *whosoever* gospel. Some verses from John are often used to refute election. Actually, no book in the whole Scripture is clearer on both absolute predestination and sovereign election.

I am the good shepherd, and know my sheep, and am known of mine. As the Father knoweth me, even so know I the Father: and I lay down my life for the sheep. And other sheep I have, which are not of this fold: them also I must bring, and they shall hear my voice; and there shall be one fold, and one shepherd (John 10:14–16).

These words cannot be understood without accepting the truth of unconditional election. Our Lord here speaks of certain people who belonged to him even though at that very moment they were lost—"Other sheep I *have*." Notice the following things clearly taught in this text: (1) Christ calls some people "his sheep" long before he saves them. They belong to him at that very moment even though they are lost. (2) He declares that he "must, and surely will, find and bring them safely into the one true fold." Not a single sheep will be left not found. (3) Our Lord is positive that every one of those sheep "will hear his voice" and will come to him. That is sovereign grace choosing and bringing particular individuals to faith in Christ.

My dear friend, that is absolute sovereign election pure and simple. Look at some other texts in our Lord's prayer in the 17th Chapter of John. Notice the same expression is used time and again.

John 17:2: As thou hast given him power over all flesh, that he should give eternal life to *as many as thou hast given him.*

John 17:6: I have manifested thy name unto the men *which thou gavest me out of the world:* thine they were, and *thou gavest them me;* and they have kept thy word.

John 17:9: I pray for them: I pray *not for the world,* but for *them which thou hast given me;* for they are thine.

John 17:11: And now I am no more in the world, but these are in the world, and I come to thee. Holy Father, keep through thine own name *those whom thou hast given me,* that they may be one, as we are.

John 17:12a: While I was with them in the world, I kept them in thy name: *those that thou gavest me* I have kept. . .

John 17:24: Father, I will that they also, *whom thou hast given me,* be with me where I am; that they may behold my glory, *which thou hast given me:* for thou lovest me before the foundation of the world.

Six times in our Lord's high priestly prayer, he refers to a group of people who have been "given to him" by the Father. Christ specifically says in verse nine that he does *not pray for the world,* but for the elect who have been chosen out of the world and given to him as his sheep. Can anyone believe that Christ would die for an individual and then not pray for that individual?

Look at one more passage in the Gospel of John. This is a key verse. It is probably the most misquoted, next to Romans 8:28, of any verse in the Bible. Many evangelists use this verse in every service when they give an altar call. The problem is that they only quote half of the verse. They begin in the middle and ignore the first part. Here is the entire verse:

> All that the Father giveth me shall come to me; and him that cometh to me I will in no wise cast out (John 6:37).

Notice that the verse contains one complete sentence with two distinct but vitally connected statements. Both statements contain a specific Bible truth. The statements are related to each other as cause and effect. As I mentioned, evangelists quote only the second half. They say, with arms outstretched while inviting people to come to the front of the church, "Jesus said, 'Him that cometh to me I will in no wise cast out.'" Unfortunately they give the impression that "coming to Christ" and coming to the front are one and the same thing. It is true that Jesus said "him that cometh to me I will in no wise cast out," but he said those words as a conclusion to the first statement. Why can we be certain that everyone who comes to Christ will be accepted? Because those who come do so only because they already are one of his sheep. They come only because the Father is drawing them and he is drawing them because he has given them to Christ in eternal covenant. The "coming ones" and the "given ones" are one and the same people. Those who believe in the free will of man (Arminians) will not freely preach the first part of John 6:37, which is unconditional election, and a Hyper-Calvinist will not preach the second part of the verse, which is the free and universal proclamation of the gospel. We must preach both parts of this verse, and I might add, preach them both with equal enthusiasm and in the given order.

"All that the Father giveth me shall come to me..." is the truth of sovereign election. It is assuring us that there will be no empty houses in heaven catching cobwebs because someone was not willing to "claim by faith what Christ purchased for them." No, no, my friend, every chosen one will be there. The Shepherd will seek, find, and save each one of his chosen sheep. After all, his reputation as a Shepherd is at stake as well as the Father's purpose and glory.

The second part of the verse, "...and him that cometh to me I will in no wise cast out," is the message to a world of lost sinners. It matters not who you are, what you are, or what you have done; come to Christ and you will be received. If you do not feel ready, come anyway, and you will be received. You say you have not felt your sin enough. Where, I ask, does the text say anything about feeling your sin enough? It says, "Come!" and assures all who come, regardless of their inadequacy, that they will be received.

People often ask, "Pastor, how can you reconcile election and the free proclamation of the gospel? How do you get those two things together?" I tell them that you never have to reconcile friends; you only reconcile enemies, and the free preaching of the gospel is not an enemy of sovereign election. The two doctrines are friends. As to getting them together, I insist that the Holy Spirit himself has put those two things together in John 6:37. The real question is, "How dare you try to separate them!" How dare anyone seek to put asunder what God has joined together?

The Apostle Paul taught sovereign election.

One entire chapter in Paul's letter to the Romans deals with the absolute sovereignty of God in election. We will look at that chapter in detail when we cover some objections to election. The following text cannot be understood except as teaching sovereign election unto salvation.

> But we are bound to give thanks alway to God for you, brethren beloved of the Lord, because God hath from the beginning chosen you to salvation through sanctification of the Spirit and belief of the truth (2 Thess. 2:13).

Notice how the NIV translates the same verse.

> But we ought always to thank God for you, brothers loved by the Lord, because from the beginning God chose you to be saved through the sanctifying work of the Spirit and through belief in the truth (2 Thess. 2:13).

You may have difficulty grasping this truth, but we dare not retreat and run away from God's Word. Read these words carefully, think about them, and ask the Lord to help you see and believe what they mean. *Don't ever be afraid of looking at the Word of God!* Don't ever take an attitude that refuses to look at passages that are "controversial." There are some who treat certain subjects in a manner that infers the Holy Spirit made a mistake by putting such "controversial issues" into the Scripture in the first place.

Don't run from any verse of Scripture even if you do not understand it! Let's look carefully at this particular text.

First of all, *Paul specifically states that election is "unto salvation."* In Bible school I was taught that election was true, but had nothing to do with salvation. You choose to be saved with your free will, and then God sovereignly chooses where he wants you to serve. You could not force that idea into this text with a sledgehammer. The Holy Spirit says that election is unto personal *salvation*. God chose us "unto salvation," or as the NIV says, "to be *saved."* What can be clearer!

Secondly, *we are to give thanks to God for choosing us.* Election is always mentioned in the context of joy. *"Blessed* be ...God...he hath *chosen* us..." (Eph. 1:3, 4). "Blessed is the man whom thou *choosest,* and *causest* to approach unto thee..." (Psalm 65:4a). If the truth of sovereign election does not thrill your heart, then you either do not have a clue as to what it really means or your heart is spiritually dead! Nowhere are we told to praise man for making a decision. No, no, we are to give thanks to God for every man's conversion, not praise to the man for his choice. Look at the text.

Thirdly, the text tells us *why it is necessary that we preach election.* People say to me, "Why do you preach about election when you know some people do not agree to it?" I always reply, "I do not have any choice. The Bible says I am 'bound to.' I have to preach election and give thanks to God for election or I am deliberately disobeying this text."

Sometimes these people say, "But why do you have to preach about election so often?" Now, I really don't preach on the subject often, but preaching election one time is too much for the person who does not believe it. Again, I refer them to this same text. Notice Paul says, "We ought *always* to thank God" for choosing you. I remember a man in one congregation who really disliked me simply because I believed and preached election. His daughter got converted but he still disliked me. The boy she was dating got converted and the man still did not like me. I had the joy of marrying this young couple and during the ceremony I asked them both, "Do you believe that God in his sovereign purposes chose you for each other, and do you confess that his sovereign plan brought about this event this day?" After the service the man was livid with anger. he said, "You can't even perform a wedding ceremony without talking about the sovereignty of God."

I believe we should preach sovereignty, pray and thank God for sovereignty, sing about sovereignty, and practice our belief in sovereignty in all we do. What else can James mean when he says:

> Go to now, ye that say, To day or to morrow we will go into such a city, and continue there a year, and buy and sell, and get gain...For that ye ought to say, If the Lord will, we shall live, and do this, or that. But now ye rejoice in your boastings: all such rejoicing is evil (James 4:13, 15–16).

Is not James accusing us of actual sin when we speak about our wills controlling things by failing to acknowledge the sovereign control of God over all things? "Rejoicing in our boastings" in this text is nothing less than thinking, speaking, and acting as if the events of tomorrow are in our hands and are our choices alone.

The fourth thing to note in the verse (2 Thess. 2:13) is the rest of the verse plus the following verses. Let me quote the whole section:

> But we are bound to give thanks alway to God for you, brethren beloved of the Lord, because God hath from the beginning chosen you to salvation through sanctification of the Spirit and belief of the truth: Whereunto he called you by our gospel, to the obtaining of the glory of our Lord Jesus Christ. Therefore, brethren, stand fast, and hold the traditions which ye have been taught, whether by word, or our epistle (2 Thess. 2:13–15).

Paul tells us that God not only chose us to salvation but he also explains the means that God used to accomplish his goal. We were saved "through, first of all, the sanctifying work of the Holy Spirit." That is talking about regeneration giving us a new heart enabling us to sincerely want to believe. This is more properly covered under the doctrine of regeneration. Secondly, we were also saved through "the belief of the truth" (verse 13b). We must be born of God in order to be able to believe, and we must believe in order to be saved. In other words, the God who chooses us to be saved guarantees salvation will happen by his sending the Holy Spirit to quicken us in regeneration. He also sends the gospel so we hear and believe it. God ordains the means to the end as well the end itself. 2 Thessalonians 2:13 is truly a powerful text of Scripture.

Probably no verse teaching election is as well known as Ephesians 1:3, 4. Let us examine it.

> Blessed be the God and Father of our Lord Jesus Christ, who hath blessed us with all spiritual blessings in heavenly places in Christ: According as he

hath chosen us in him before the foundation of the world, that we should be holy and without blame before him in love: (Eph. 1:3, 4).

This text is clear and shows that in whatever sense the nation of Israel was "chosen" to be God's earthly nation, the church was "chosen" as the special spiritual people of God (cf. Ex. 19:5, 6 and 1 Pet. 2:9–10). Please note that God chose us in eternity, or before we were even born!

Peter taught the doctrine of election

The following two verses both speak about the foreknowledge of God.

Peter, an apostle of Jesus Christ, to the strangers scattered throughout Pontus, Galatia, Cappadocia, Asia, and Bithynia, Elect according to the foreknowledge of God the Father, through sanctification of the Spirit, unto obedience and sprinkling of the blood of Jesus Christ...(1 Pet 1:1–2a).

Forasmuch as ye know that ye were not redeemed with corruptible things, as silver and gold, from your vain conversation received by tradition from your fathers; But with the precious blood of Christ, as of a lamb without blemish and without spot: Who verily was foreordained before the foundation of the world, but was manifest in these last times for you, (1 Pet 1:18–20).

One of the objections to our view of election is that "Election is all based foreknowledge," and then foreknowledge, as just mentioned, is defined as meaning "prior knowledge," or God's ability to "see into the future and make decisions based on that foreseen information." God is said to have purposed to choose us because he foresaw that we would choose him. If you will do a careful word study of "foreknowledge" you will see that the word really means "fore-loved" or "sovereignly chose." For now, look carefully at the above two verses from Peter.

The NIV translates 1 Pet.1:1–2: "To God's elect...who have been chosen..." You can see that the NIV understands the word *foreknown* to mean, *fore-loved* or *chosen*. We quoted both verses deliberately. We have a question for those who wish to argue that God's reason for choosing us was based on his looking forward into history to see what we would do and then basing his action of choosing us on that foreseen information. Would anyone dare say the same thing about 'the foreordination of Christ' in verse 20? Can anyone seriously believe that God purposed, or chose, to give Christ up to the death of the cross only because he, the Father, looked into the future and "foresaw" that Christ would be willing to die, and, on the basis of that prior information, he decided to send Christ into the world to die? No! No! That is nonsense. Acts 2:22–24 is crystal clear that the Father consciously and deliberately foreordained the death of his Son. Well, the idea about God choosing us because he foresaw our faith is just as much nonsense. In whatever sense Christ was 'foreordained to die,' I was 'foreordained to be saved!' It is just that simple.

God's foreknowledge of the Church is like an architect's foreknowledge of a building. Would anyone say that a building is like it is because the architect had the ability to see into the future? He 'foresaw' that Contractor A would get the brick contract. Since Contractor A liked white bricks instead of red ones, the architect put white bricks into the plan. He also 'foresaw' that Contractor B would get the lighting contract and then used in the plans the kind of lights he 'foresaw' that Contractor B would select. Because the architect had perfect foreknowledge of every contractor and exactly what specific thing each would use, he was able to design a building exactly like the one he knew all the contractors would build. You laugh at such an absurd idea, and so you should. You will say, "That architect knew exactly what that building was going to be like down to the last nail simply because he was the one who designed it. The contractors built the way they did only because the architect designed it that way. My dear friend, the Church is exactly the same. God had perfect foreknowledge of the Church for exactly the same reason. God did not need any foreknowledge to design and plan the church any more than an architect needs foreknowledge to design a building. God knew who would be saved because he sovereignly chose them to be saved.

How God taught me sovereign election

God used a Mennonite farmer in a small country church near Lancaster, Pennsylvania, to open my eyes and heart to see and believe that sovereign election is a biblical truth. This man was in charge of the Wednesday evening Bible study and was going through the Gospel of John. In the providence of God, he had started to study A.W. Pink's commentary on that book. The following verses were being discussed that particular evening:

> Then came the Jews round about him, and said unto him, 'How long dost thou make us to doubt? If thou be the Christ, tell us plainly.' Jesus answered them, 'I told you, and ye believed not: the works that I do in my Father's name, they bear witness of me. But ye believe not! because ye are not of my

sheep, as I said unto you. My sheep hear my voice, and I know them, and they follow me:' (John 10:24–27).

The teacher had two pieces of poster board which he set on separate chairs. On one poster board were written the words *heard and believed* and on the other the words *heard and believed not*. The two chairs, thus labeled, represented the two groups of people spoken of in the verses being studied. Three questions were asked and each one was answered by the words of Christ addressed to these Jews. The questions dealt with why some believed and why the others would not believe. The teacher's primary concern was to show the real reason that made the difference between the two groups. Why did some "hear and believe" and others "hear and believe not"? What made the vital difference between the two groups?

First question: "Why did the first group *refuse to* believe the gospel?" The teacher turned the first card over and written on the back was the word *goat*. The Savior's words in verse twenty-six were unmistakably clear. "Ye believe not *because ye are not of my sheep."* It was impossible to argue about the meaning of such a concise statement. Why did they not believe? Christ gave the answer, "Because ye are not of my sheep." In other words, if they would have been his sheep instead of goats, they would have heard and believed. The fact that they would not believe proved they were goats and not sheep. Our Lord had earlier taught the same truth. In fact, his words in verse twenty-five, "I told you, and ye believed not..." probably refers back to John 8 where Jesus said unto them, "...If ye were Abraham's children, ye would do the works of Abraham...Ye do the deeds of your father...If God were your Father, ye would love me: for I proceeded forth and came from God;...Why do ye not understand my speech? *even because ye cannot hear my words*... Ye are of your father the Devil..." (John 8:39–44). These people not only did not believe, but Christ said they *could not believe*. Why? They were not "of the Father." They were not "Abraham's seed." They were, in other words, not one of *God's elect*. They were not one of his sheep.

This does not mean that they wanted to believe but Christ would not allow them to do so. One of the wicked caricatures of our view states, "Many people want to be saved but God refuses to save them because they are not elect." That is as big a lie as anyone ever told. We believe and preach that God has, does, and always will, save every sinner without a single exception that comes to him in the name of Christ! No, no, this verse means that they were totally unable to even *want* to believe because of their depravity, and God had sovereignly and justly chosen to leave them in that state. You can see in both John 10:26 and 8:39–44 the same "if" and "would have" relationship. Who and what these people *were* determined what they did or did not do. Our teacher reminded us that we all, without exception, were born with that same nature and into that same state of sin and unbelief.

Second question: "Why did the second group hear and believe?" The teacher turned over the second card and it had the word *sheep* written on it. This question logically followed the first one and again the Savior's word gave a clear answer. Verse twenty-seven said, "My sheep hear my voice…" The teacher kept contrasting the two cards representing the two groups. "The gospel came to all of them, but one group believed and the other group would not. Why? What made the difference in the two groups? Why did the group called "my sheep" hear and believe? Did they have better hearts? Stronger wills? Keener minds? No, they believed because they were sheep.

I got the message! The "heard and believed" group did so only because they were "sheep" and the "heard and would not believe" group did not believe because they were not sheep; they were goats. Now I had always known the Bible divided men into two classes: sheep and goats. I also knew that the sheep were God's people and the goats were not. However, I never knew until that night why some people were sheep and others were not, and more specifically, that I had believed the gospel only because I had been chosen to be a sheep in eternity. It was always clear, as the poster cards showed, that "sheep" and "hear and believed" belonged together, and likewise "goat" and "would not hear and believe" went together. However, no one had ever shown me which was the cause and which was the effect. I had thought, as my free will teachers had carefully taught me, that I had decided to change my goat nature into a sheep nature by an act of my "free will." Oh, how those who love free will would like to make John 10:26 say, "You are not my sheep because you are unwilling to believe; if you would be willing to believe you would become one of my sheep." Ah, my friend, the text clearly says the opposite. Jesus said, "You believe not *because* you are not my sheep!"

The farmer's third question opened up the whole truth of God's sovereign election and forever silenced the nonsense of free will as the decisive factor in my "hearing and believing." The third question:

John G. Reisinger

"According to our Lord's words in verses twenty-six and twenty-seven, *does hearing and believing make you a sheep, or do you hear and believe because you have already been chosen to be a sheep?*" In an instant, God assured my heart of the answer. I knew which was the cause and which was the effect. The words of Christ were clear as crystal. The Spirit of God assured me that I had heard the Shepherd's voice only because I had previously been chosen to be one of his sheep. I had willingly come to Christ only because I belonged to Christ by his sovereign election and he was claiming, by his power, in time, what had been given to him in eternity. I was not a goat that had become a sheep by a decision of my so-called free will, but rather, I was a lost sheep that had been found! And I had been found only because I was a chosen to be sheep from eternity. A goat had not become a sheep; rather a lost sheep had become a found sheep.

Christ did not become my Shepherd when he brought me to faith and repentance. He sought, found, and brought me to himself in salvation only because the Father, in eternity, had given me to him to be one of his sheep. That word "because" in verse twenty-six forever settled the reason of why some people reject the gospel. "My sheep hear" in verse twenty-seven could only mean that I had heard and believed because I was a sheep from eternity. The texts can mean nothing else! Put down in your *Book of Indisputable Facts* these two things: (1) Only those who have been eternally chosen to be sheep will ever come to Christ, and (2) every one of the sheep, without a single exception, will come when Christ draws them.

My mind was flooded with this amazing truth. *I was one of God's elect from eternity!* Why had I heard and believed the gospel? I knew the answer. Only because I had been chosen in Christ before the foundation of the world. I was not redeemed because I had believed, but rather the One who had redeemed me before I was born had now found me and revealed himself to me. Christ had sought me because I was his property. I did not become his sheep when he found me, but he had sought me and found me because I was one of his lost sheep.

As I left that little church in Lancaster County, I looked up into the heavens with tears in my eyes. I knew that before a single star had ever shown a beam of light, God had sovereignly chosen me as a sheep and purposed to draw me to himself and give me faith. With a heart filled with amazement and praise, I gladly acknowledged that I owed every part of my salvation to God's grace in sovereign election. I knew I was in possession of eternal life only because the Father had chosen me, the Savior had died for me, and the Holy Spirit had given me faith and a new heart.

Thus far we have covered the textual proof that the Bible clearly teaches the truth of God's sovereign unconditional election, the precise points of difference among sincere Christians on this subject, the basic meaning of the word *chose*, the doctrine of election in both the Old and New Testament Scriptures, our Lord's and the Apostle's uniform teaching on election, and lastly, how God taught me the truth of his electing grace.

We now want to clear away some gross caricatures or misconceptions. Some of these arguments demonstrate that many sincere saints have never heard the truth of election clearly taught, and unfortunately, some of the caricatures are deliberate, wicked, and willful distortions of God's clear truth by people who really know better. The former group is often Godly saints who need to be taught. The latter are wolves in sheep's clothing whose hearts have never been changed by sovereign grace. These people need to bow to God in true humility and repentance and be converted.

Election is not the Gospel

The first misconception confuses the doctrine of election with the gospel message. There are some men who think that preaching election is preaching the gospel. It is true that no one would ever be saved if there were no sovereign election, but it is just as true that preaching election alone will not convert sinners. We believe election is what makes the gospel work but we do not believe that election is the gospel. When the jailer asked Paul, "What must I do to be saved?" the Apostle did not say, "Believe in the doctrine of election and you will be saved." When Paul, in 1 Corinthians 15:1–4, gave a summary of the gospel that he preached, he did not mention the word *election*. Many well-meaning preachers whose motives I do not question are actually doing more harm than good by trying to exalt God's sovereign electing grace as the gospel itself.

I know of no verse that teaches election any more clearly than Acts 13:48. However, that text does not set forth the gospel message. Look at what is said:

> And when the Gentiles heard this, they were glad, and glorified the word of the Lord: and as many as were ordained to eternal life believed (Acts 13:48).

It is essential that we notice that Luke is not preaching a gospel sermon, but he is giving a *report* of what happened earlier that day when Paul had preached the gospel. The first part of the chapter is the evangelistic message referred to by the words "when the Gentiles heard *this.*" The heart of the gospel message, found in verses 37–40, is the apostolic gospel. It involves telling sinners about the death, burial, and resurrection of Christ and then assuring them that all who believe that message will be forgiven of every sin. Verse 48 is the report of the results, or effects, the Holy Spirit accomplished through the preached gospel earlier that day.

How different was the reporting done by the Apostles than that which is done by the 'evangelists' of our day. The Apostles gave God all the credit for every conversion. The apostles "glorified the Word of the Lord" because they knew that the Word of the Lord alone had produced the amazing results. Today the report would read quite differently. An evangelist would boast, "I had ten first-time decisions today," or, "twenty people opened their hearts and gave God a chance to save them." The statistical boasting today is a result of men wrongly believing that conversion is effected by a combination of the power of a sinner's free will and the "soul winning ability" of a preacher. The apostles knew nothing of such man-exalting and God-denying nonsense. They always credited God's sovereign electing grace with being the cause of every sinner's faith.

It amazes me to see the lengths that men will go in attempting to deny the truth of God's sovereign electing grace. Kenneth Taylor, in his *Living Bible*, which is marketed as a translation even though it is really a paraphrase, translates Acts 13:48b this way: "…as many as wanted eternal life, believed." In the margin he gives "disposed to" as an alternative meaning for "wanted." He then gives "ordained to" as a third option. It is not possible to make the verse say, "As many as *wanted,* believed." This is not paraphrasing in order to better understand the truth; this is radically and deliberately changing the meaning in order to hide the truth. If "were disposed to" is a legitimate translation, which it is not, it would still not settle the question as to why those particular individuals were disposed to believe, or who was responsible for disposing them. The word *ordained* as a third option shows that Taylor knows what the text means. It also shows his total bias against the truth of sovereign grace by passing off his interpretation as translation.

Spurgeon answered Taylor's distortion long before it was ever made. The great Baptist preacher explained Act 13:48 well:

> Attempts have been made to prove that these words do not teach predestination, but these attempts so clearly do violence that I will not waste time in answering them... I read, "As many as were ordained to eternal life believed," and I shall not twist that text but shall glorify the grace of God by ascribing to it every man's faith...Is it not God Who gives the disposition to believe? If men are disposed to have eternal life, does not he in every case dispose them? Is it wrong for God to give grace? If it be right for him to give it, is it wrong for him to PURPOSE to give it? Would you have him give it by accident? If it is right for him to purpose to give grace today, it was right for him to purpose it before that date—and, since he changes not—from eternity.

A.W. Pink's comments are just as clear and concise:

> Every artifice of human ingenuity has been employed to blunt the sharp edge of this Scripture and to explain away the obvious meaning of these words, but it has been employed in vain, though nothing will ever be able to reconcile this and similar passages to the mind of natural man. "As many as were ordained to eternal life believed."

There are four things we can learn. First, that believing is the consequence and not the cause of God's decree. Second, we can see that a limited number only are "ordained to eternal life," for if all men without exception were thus ordained by God, then the words "as many as" would be a meaningless qualification. Third, this "ordination" of God is not to mere external privilege but to "eternal life," not to service but to salvation itself. Fourth, we understand that that all of the "as many as," not one less—who are thus ordained by God to eternal life, will most certainly believe."

Again, I remind you that election is not the gospel, but is what makes the gospel work. If there were no sovereign election, we could preach the gospel until our tongues fell off and not one single soul would be saved. Likewise, we could preach and teach election every Sunday for a lifetime, but unless we also preached the gospel facts, not one conversion would take place. We must understand that a man may preach a great sermon on election and never preach the gospel; and likewise, he may preach a clear gospel message without mentioning election. However, we must hasten to add, that first of all, no true biblical gospel sermon will ever say, or in any way infer, anything that denies or contradicts the truth of sovereign election, and secondly, no biblical sermon on election will ever deny or contradict either the gospel or its free and unfettered preaching to all sinners.

"But election isn't fair!"

Some years ago, I was at a weekend retreat with a group of university students. During a discussion period, someone raised the subject of predestination and election. One girl asked, "Where does the Bible clearly teach that God sovereignly chooses some people to be saved?" I asked her to read Romans 9 aloud. She paused a second with a surprised look on her face as she slowly read, "Before they were born or had done good or evil." When she got to 9:13b and read, "Jacob have I loved, but, Esau have I hated," she stopped and said, "But that's not fair." I asked her to read the next verse. The King James Version says, "What shall we say then? Is there unrighteousness with God? God forbid." She had a modern speech translation and it said, "You will object and say, 'but that's not fair.'" The surprised girl blurted out, "That's what I just said!"

Now listen very carefully. If you object to election on the grounds that you think it is unfair, you are using an objection that has *already been used and answered* in the Scripture. The moment you say, "Election is unfair," you are admitting that you disagree with Paul's teaching in Romans 9:11–13 because that is the very objection he is presupposing his opponents will make. In his answer, Paul does not back up or soften his statement. He declares that God has every right to show mercy to whomever he chooses.

The young lady continued to read Romans 9. She read verse 18, "Therefore hath he mercy on whom he will have mercy, and whom he will he hardeneth." She literally gasped, "Then man cannot be held responsible. He is only a robot." Again I asked her to read the next verse. The King James says, "Thou wilt say then unto me, why doth he yet find fault? For who hath resisted his will?" The young lady's modern speech translation read, "You will say to me, 'Then man cannot be held responsible. He is only a robot.'" The poor girl said, "I did it again!" Let me repeat what I just said. If you object to election on the grounds that you think it makes man a robot, you are using an objection that has *already been used and answered* in the Scripture. The moment you say, "Election means man cannot be held responsible," you are admitting that you disagree with Paul's teaching in Romans 9:18. Again, we see that Paul did not soften his statement. He declares that the Potter has the sovereign right to fashion, as he chooses, the lump of clay, which is sinful man.

Both of the above objections forget the fall of Adam and the doctrine of depravity. They treat sinners as if God created them sinful instead of remembering that we all chose, in Adam, to sin. Let me try to illustrate how ridiculous these objections are.

Suppose a very wealthy lady in your town chooses to adopt two or three orphans. She gives them her name, her love, and her fortune. Everybody in town would automatically accuse her of being mean and unfair because she only adopted three orphans instead of ten! You know that would not happen. Everyone would applaud her for adopting two or three simply because she did *not have to adopt any!* However, let God choose *some* sinners, when he could justly by-pass all sinners since he owes no sinner anything but death, and God somehow becomes unfair or mean. In the case of the wealthy lady and the orphans, we magnify her gracious act. In the case of God and sinners, some will ignore his grace and vilify his character.

The writers of Scripture say very little about the dark side of election, called reprobation, simply because they are not at all surprised that God justly leaves some sinners to perish. The biblical authors are constantly amazed that God chose *anyone to be saved,* and even more amazed that he sovereignly *chose them.*

Since the objection of "unfairness" is so common and easily appeals to sentimentality, we need to say a bit more about it. A good friend of mine was covering the subject of election while teaching a high school and college class in Sunday School. There were seven kids in the class. My friend, Bob Dittmar, took an envelope out of his pocket and said, "There is a one dollar bill in this envelope. I am going to choose one of you seven and give it to you as a gift. Do I have the right to choose anyone of the seven?" All seven vocally agreed that it was his money and he could do with it as he chose. Bob handed the envelope to a boy and he opened it, took out the dollar and said, "Thank you." Bob asked the other six how they felt about not getting the dollar and none of them were upset. They, of course, would have been happy if they had been chosen but were not upset since it was "his money to do with as he chose."

Bob then got two more envelopes out of his pocket and gave them to two girls. The girls opened the envelopes, took out a dollar and said, "Thank you." When asked how they felt, the other four said, "Something does not ring right about all this." The three with envelopes insisted that all was fair and right since it was Bob's money and he did not owe any of them anything. My friend then gave three more kids envelopes and now six of the seven kids each had a dollar. He asked the one person out of the seven who had no envelope how she felt and she immediately replied, "I was cheated. It was not fair." The other six young people all reminded the girl how she had agreed that the teacher had a right to choose anyone since he owed none of them anything. It was a free gift and she could not accuse Bob of being unfair. They really ganged up on her and put her down. They were all firm believers in Bob's right to "sovereignly choose" since it was his money and he owed none of them anything.

Bob then gave the last girl an envelope and when she opened it, she discovered a *five-dollar* bill. Guess what the other six all cried. "It's not fair! I was cheated!" My friend said, "Aren't you the same people who were just arguing that I could not possibly cheat this girl since I owed her nothing? How can I all of the sudden cheat you when you just said I owed you nothing? Besides, you are holding a dollar as a gift you did not earn or deserve."

I am sure you can see that the "it is not fair" argument is utterly ridiculous. What makes the situation even worse is the fact that God freely offers to give sinners a full pardon for all sin if they would only be willing to receive it; but they all, without exception apart from his sovereign grace, say, "No."

Why does God predestinate some people to go to hell?

The answer to this misconception is simple. HE DOESN'T! God does not predestinate people to go to hell. This is a straw dummy that preachers who reject election often erect. Instead of dealing with the verses of Scripture that we show them, they make statements like the above. All we need ask is this: "Did not anyone ever tell you about a man named Adam and how he used his free will to choose sin and plunge his whole posterity into depravity." How can God possibly predestinate someone to go to hell who is already on his *way to hell by the choice of his own "free will?"* The coming of Christ has absolutely nothing to do with people going to hell. It only affects people going to heaven. All men were lost long before Christ came. His death has nothing to do with any man's condemnation. If Christ had never come and died, all men would have justly perished in hell. How can his coming and dying have anything to do with the sons of Adam being lost sinners? Ask the question this way: "Why does God predestinate some SINNERS to go to hell" and you have a whole new discussion.

Election sends no one to hell, but it does get some people into heaven. We could bring up from hell sinners who are now there, or who will ever be there, and not a single one of them would blame election for their being in hell. The so-called pagan who supposedly "never heard" will say, "My testimony is recorded in Romans 1. I did not follow the light God gave me nor did I follow my conscience. I deliberately pushed away the truth. In my heart, I knew when I cut down a tree and used half of it to build a fire and the other half to carve an idol that it was the same wood."

The Jew will say, "I am in hell because I would not obey the light that God gave my nation. I trusted in the fact that I was a Jew and would not repent and believe the gospel promises of a Redeemer." We could go on and on and listen to one testimony after another and every lost sinner would blame his or her own wicked heart for their lost estate. There will never be a single soul in hell who will say, "I wanted to be saved from sin but God would not save me because I was not one of the elect." The very throne of grace would collapse and be destroyed if that were true.

However, we must quickly add that the reverse is true for those in heaven. Bring any one of the saints who praise our God day and night from heaven and not a single one will say, "I am here because of my free will. I am feasting on the riches and glories of grace because I decided to let Jesus save me." No, no, the uniform song from heaven will forever more be:

> 'Tis not that I did choose thee, for, Lord that could not be;
> This heart would still refuse thee, hadst thou not chosen me.
> Thou from the sin that stained me hast cleansed and set me free;
> of old thou hast ordained me, that I should live to thee.
>
> 'Twas sov 'reign mercy called me and taught my op 'ning mind;
> the world had else enthralled me, to heav 'nly glories blind.
> My heart owns none before thee, for thy rich grace I thirst;
> this knowing, if I love thee, thou must have loved me first.

But election is based on God's foreknowledge

This is the favorite argument of the "Bible believing fundamentalist" of our generation. "Oh, yes, God indeed chooses some sinners to be saved, but his choice is based on the fact that he foresees which sinner will be willing to accept the gospel. God then, on the basis of this foreknown information, chooses those who are willing to choose him. Romans 8:29 makes this very clear." This is like a big rug that Arminians use to sweep the truth of election under. The problem is the big lump in the rug that cannot be hidden!

First of all, I agree that God indeed has the ability to look into the future. However, he has never yet found anyone with a willingness to believe. There is no "foreseen faith" to see. Romans 3:11, 12 tell us exactly what God foresaw:

> There is none that understandeth, there is none that seeketh after God. They are all gone out of the way, they are together become unprofitable; there is none that doeth good, no, not one (Rom 3:11–12).

It is impossible to find some way for God to foresee a willingness of someone to seek God in the crowd Paul describes in these verses. There is *none*, and that really means *no, not one,* who is willing to seek God until God first seeks him. The only faith that God foresees in any man is the faith that he himself purposes to give that man.

Foreknowledge is not an attribute of God that gives him the ability to see into the future. He of course can do that. When the Bible says that God foreknows it means God purposes *to do something.* Foreknowledge is an *act of God,* not merely God having prior knowledge of something that will happen in the future. God only 'foresees' what is absolutely certain to happen, and not one single thing can be absolutely certain to happen unless God has chosen to fix it so it does happen. Nothing happens that is not part of God's foreordained plan.

It is impossible for anyone, even God, to foreknow for certain that something is going to happen unless it is certain that it will actually happen. There can be absolutely no possible contingencies that will keep it from happening if it is truly foreknown. That is why you and I cannot foreknow one single thing in the future for certain. We cannot perfectly control any of the contingencies and we have no control at all over many of them. Many unknowns may keep our plans and purposes from happening. God alone foreknows, simply because he alone can fix any given thing so it will positively happen. God does control every contingency. This is why Romans 8:28 is such a comfort. If man has a true "free will," then even God could not be absolutely certain of any event since the man might change his mind at the last second.

The word *know* basically means *to love*. Look at the following texts of Scripture.

> You only have I known of all the families of the earth: therefore I will punish you for all your iniquities (Amos 3:2).

It is obvious that God "knew all things about every single nation," but he *knew*, or *loved*, Israel in a special way. This text means that God knew, loved, or chose Israel alone out of all the other nations.

> But if any man love God, the same is known of him (1 Cor. 8:3).

In this text *love* and *known* are used interchangeably.

> And then will I profess unto them, I never knew you: depart from me, ye that work iniquity (Matt. 7:23).

This verse cannot possibly mean that Jesus did not "know all about" the people to whom he was speaking. It was because he did know all about them that they were rejected. He knows everything about every nation and every person. Jesus is saying that he did not know them *in a way of love*. He did not love them redemptively. There is a sense in which it is not nearly as important that we know the Lord as it is that *he knows us!*

> For the LORD knoweth the way of the righteous: but the way of the ungodly shall perish (Psalm 1:6).

Again it is obvious that God sees and knows everything the ungodly do just as much as he sees and knows what the godly do. However, God *knows*, or watches over *in love*, the way of the righteous.

We could produce many other texts that clearly prove that the word *know* means *love*. When God knows someone, it means he loves that person. When he "fore" knows someone, foreloves them. The word *foreknow* really means the same thing as *choose* or *elect*. God's "fore" knowledge is his "fore" love, or his sovereign choice of a person. When God foreknows a person, he knows them in a way of special electing love. It means that he chooses them unto salvation.

In the next chapter, we want to show the effects the doctrine of election had on the life and ministry of the Apostle Paul.

Shortly after I came to understand the truth of sovereign grace, I did a study of the effect of the doctrine of election on the life and ministry of Paul. I tried to look up and analyze every reference Paul made to election, predestination, calling, etc. I was amazed at how Paul's life and ministry not only clearly established the truth of sovereign grace; but it also totally refuted most of the objections that people offer to election and predestination. Here is what I discovered.

Paul attributed his own conversion, and the conversion of all of his converts, to God's sovereign election!

Paul never once mentioned the so-called free will of man when talking about anyone's conversion. He never considered the will of man the decisive factor in anyone's salvation. This is not to say that man does not have to be willing to believe, but it does mean that Paul viewed that willingness as a gift from God and not a product of man's so-called free will. Notice the great joy Paul expresses as he gives the right person the deserved credit for salvation. He always praises God's sovereign electing grace for every conversion.

First of all, he praised God for *his own conversion*. Paul's conversion experience is recorded several places in Acts and his epistles. In every case, God is credited from beginning to end as the reason Paul is saved. Notice one instance of his testimony:

> But when it *pleased God,* who separated me from my mother's womb, and *called me* by his grace, To *reveal his Son in me,* that I might preach him among the heathen; immediately *I conferred not with flesh and blood* (Gal. 1:15–16).

Notice how strikingly different that statement is from the "I decided to give Jesus a chance," or the "I'm glad I was willing to let God save me," kind of testimonies we hear today. Notice the following things: (1) Paul's conversion did not take place "When I decided to accept," but *"when it pleased God."* (2) It was not when Paul decided to "open my heart and let Jesus come in," but when (a) God *"called me* [effectually, or regenerated me] by his grace," and (b) *"revealed his Son* in me." A new heart is not the result of a dead sinner's willingness to be made alive but is the direct result of a divine revelation of the Holy Spirit's power to give a dead sinner a new heart. (3) Paul did not need a personal worker or counselor to convince him that he had been converted. He did not have to "confer with flesh and blood" and be assured that "Jesus has indeed come into your heart." When the Lord of Glory takes up his abode in a poor sinner's heart, that sinner knows something amazing has happened. If a sinner has to be badgered and argued into believing that Christ has indeed "come into your heart," would we not be justified in asking if it was worth while to have such an experience?

It is interesting how insistent Paul is that his readers understand that it was not his will, but God's sovereign will and purpose, that was totally responsible for his conversion.

> But now, after that ye have known God, *or rather are known of God...* (Gal. 4:9a).

Notice that the "or rather are known of God" is a very conscious and deliberate little insertion. It is almost as if Paul was saying, "I do not want you to misunderstand. I surely believe knowing God is vital, but I know [love] God only because he first knew [loved] me." Today we might paraphrase Paul's words this way: "Just in case a 'free will' enthusiast thinks I agree with him, let me set the record straight. I believe in sovereign electing grace. I was known by God long before I knew God."

Secondly, all of his converts were saved only because of election. Paul is not at all vague about why some people responded to the gospel under his preaching and others did not. He always made it clear that when anyone was converted, God alone was to have the praise. Since Paul believed that God's sovereign electing grace was responsible for every conversion, he consciously gave God the praise for every conversion. The following text is typical:

> But we are bound to give thanks alway to God for you, brethren beloved of the Lord, because God hath from the beginning chosen you to salvation... (2 Thess. 2:13a).

The NIV translates this verse, "chose you to be saved." We looked at this verse in the first chapter. I mention it again only to prove the point that Paul never congratulates the sinner on his "wise choice" or his good sense in "accepting Christ" nor did he praise himself or some other preacher for the "great message." He credited God with the whole of every man's salvation from beginning to end, including the gift of faith.

Further, Paul not only attributed his own conversion and the conversion of all of his converts to the electing grace of God, but he did the same *for all conversions.* Acts 13:48 is a statement concerning conversion in general. Again, we noted earlier how radically different this report is from the "I had ten first time decisions last week" brag sheets published today. My purpose in quoting it again is to emphasize that this is a deliberate statement by Paul giving conscious praise to God's electing grace as the sole cause of all of the conversions that afternoon. Free will does not enter the picture.

> And when the Gentiles heard this, they were glad, and glorified the word of the Lord: and as *many as were ordained to eternal life believed* (Acts 13:48).

Predestination was the foundation of Paul's life and call to the ministry!

How strange to read what Paul says about the effect that the truth of God's sovereign electing grace had upon him and his ministry and then hear sincere Christians say, "We should not preach about election and predestination since it is a dangerous doctrine." These people are especially afraid of hurting new believers with heavy doctrine, and they are even more concerned that lost people not be discouraged by hearing about the sovereignty of God. Let me answer these two objections with Paul's own testimony. Examine the following verses carefully and you will see how unfounded these objections are.

> And I said, What shall I do, Lord? And the Lord said unto me, Arise, and go into Damascus; and there it shall be told thee of all things which are appointed for thee to do. And when I could not see for the glory of that light, being led by the hand of them that were with me, I came into Damascus. And one Ananias, a devout man according to the law, having a good report of all the Jews which dwelt there, Came unto me, and stood, and said unto me, Brother Saul, receive thy sight. And the same hour I looked up upon him. And he said, The God of our fathers hath chosen thee, that thou shouldest know his will, and see that Just One, and shouldest hear the voice of his mouth (Acts 22:10–14).

Let's make sure we get the message Paul was conveying. (1) Paul freely admits that he was not seeking after God. He was filled with blind rage against Christ and Christians and fighting them both as hard as he could. (2) He was testifying that he was blinded: spiritually by his religious ignorance, and physically by the miraculous intervention of God. (3) Jesus spoke to him from heaven. No man was ever more amazed than Paul when he learned that this 'Lord' who had struck him down was none other than the very Jesus he was persecuting. (4) Ananias said, "Receive thy sight," and Paul was able to see. There is no hint of a suggestion that Paul had to be willing to comply before he would see. This incident is a manifestation of sovereign grace and power from beginning to end. Paul says, "And the *same hour* I looked..." The *looking* by Paul did *not give* his *sight*. The looking was the *result* of *God giving* him sight by the command of Ananias.

This passage clearly answers the two objections we are discussing. First of all, it proves that the first Christian doctrine that Paul learned as a brand new convert was the doctrine of election. Notice again what Ananias said: "The God of our fathers hath *chosen thee*..." The very first truth that Paul, a brand new convert learned, was that he was saved because God had chosen him in electing grace. And, I might add, that was a truth that Paul never forgot nor did he ever cease to be amazed that it was true.

Notice the following in verse 14. (1) Paul states that he was chosen *in order to know* God's will. He did not first know that will and then decide to believe. (2) He was chosen so that he would be *able* to 'see' that Just One. He did not first see, like what he saw, and then decide to believe. (3) He was chosen to 'hear' and did not choose because he first heard and then decided to accept salvation. Isn't it amazing how carefully the Holy Spirit chooses his words?

I think the Holy Spirit is explaining that it is essential to start off one's Christian life with the clear realization that one is a child of sovereign grace. You are not your own but you have been bought with a price and he who purchased you has every right to do with you as he pleases. We did not enter into a partnership with God at conversion; we were slaves and have been purchased out of slavery. We have neither the ability nor the right to boast about either the power of our wills or our rights to make our own choices. There can be only one boss and the sooner we learn that God is that boss, the better off we will be. Paul's experience shows that God's purpose is that we learn that truth at conversion.

I believe that one of the primary reasons preachers and other church leaders are experiencing 'burn-out' can be traced to the truth we are talking about. We cannot tell sinners that they did God a favor by *allowing* him to save them and then get them to live like they owe everything to God's grace. We cannot lead a sinner to believe that he alone, with his 'free will,' was the one decisive factor in his conversion and then urge that person to feel a deep and life-changing obligation to God's sovereign grace. In other words, if we want to get ulcers, we need only 'fast-deal' sinners into making a decision that is totally designed to help them to "be happy" and then try to get those people to willingly make sacrifices that just might infringe on their happiness. We cannot get goats to act like sheep but we can surely get burned out trying. If we teach the sinner he is "the master of his fate," don't be surprised if he lives like that were true. Teach him he is a bond slave of sovereign electing grace and it is a different matter all together.

The second thing that Paul's conversion teaches us concerns election and gospel preaching. Not only was election the first Christian doctrine Paul learned, but when he was telling about his conversion, in the Acts 22:10–14 passage, *he was giving his testimony to a group of lost people.* Now that ought to close the mouth of the objector who is frightened that a lost person should never be told about election. *Paul* was not afraid to talk about election in evangelism.

I am not at all suggesting that we must talk about election every time we preach or witness to the lost. We have already emphasized that election was not the gospel or part of the gospel. Election is what makes the gospel work. However, there are times when election is the very truth that some sinners need. Nothing kills self-sufficiency like the truth of election. Nothing humbles a proud religionist like sovereign grace. How do you respond to a sinner who says, "Leave me alone; when I get ready to believe, I will believe"? I clobber them over the head with election. I tell them they cannot get ready. I press on them the truth that God does not have to send another witness to them but can leave them alone and let them go to hell for sure. Romans 9 is not a secret for only God's sheep. It is the message for every proud 'Pharaoh' in this world. It is the hammer of God that destroys the damning myth of the power and rights of one's 'free will.' Sovereign election, rightly preached, will lead men to seek grace.

Predestination was the foundation of Paul's missionary zeal to preach the gospel.

How often have we heard the cry, "If I believed election I would never witness"? Actually, if I did *not* believe election, I would not witness! If I believed that the sinner alone had the power to make God's plan of salvation work, I would realize that no one would ever be saved. "But," we are told, "preaching election will destroy all missionary effort." Again Paul's life proves this objection to be groundless. Notice first how election motivated Paul:

> Then spake the Lord to Paul in the night by a vision, Be not afraid, but speak, and hold not thy peace: For I am with thee, and no man shall set on thee to hurt thee: for I have much people in this city (Acts 18:9, 10).

We don't usually think of Paul as a man who was afraid, but here is one instance where the Holy Spirit tells us that Paul was afraid. We can imagine that the Devil was whispering in Paul's ear about how hopeless the situation was as well as how useless were Paul's efforts. "You really don't believe you can persuade anyone in that wicked city to become a Christian. You may well lose your life." And how did God encourage Paul? He used the truth of election! God said, "Paul you are safe wherever I call you to go. I have some elect in that city and they are going to respond to the gospel when I open their hearts by my power." That is the thing that motivated our Lord in John 10:14–16. Some people, very particular people, simply *must* be saved because their salvation is the determined purpose of God. Paul was willing to suffer anything and everything for that purpose to be accomplished.

> Therefore I endure all things for the elect's sakes, that they may also obtain the salvation which is in Christ Jesus with eternal glory (2 Tim. 2:10).

Why would Paul suffer for something that did not exist? Why would he endure all that he did unless he was sure of the outcome? John Patton was a missionary to the New Hebrides islands. He lost his wife and child to disease. He was nearly killed on many occasions. He labored for nearly twenty-five years with no 'success.' Do you think he ever felt discouraged? Do you think the Devil ever whispered in his ear as he did Paul's? What would keep someone preaching in such a situation? John Patton stood over the grave of his wife and child and prayed, "Father, you have chosen a people out of every tribe and tongue to be saved. Some of those chosen ones are on this island and I will not leave until they are safely in the fold." That is what biblical election will do for missions. In God's time Patton saw the island swept into the kingdom of God. It was the doctrine of election that kept Patton on that island all that time.

I freely admit that the truth of God's electing grace, and the absolute necessity of the Holy Spirit to enable a person to be able to believe, will kill a lot of fleshly zeal that has hatched up some very 'successful' carnal methods of 'getting decisions' (and the sooner such practices are killed the better), but I assure you that both the Bible and history testify that election is the only thing that can produce and maintain true gospel mission work. Many sincere people have gone to the mission field with genuine pity and human love for those "poor people who are just waiting to hear the gospel" and after two break-ins of their homes, the loss of their possessions and constant threats to their lives, they have changed their minds and feelings about "those poor people."

Let me note one more passage that proves that believing in election did not adversely affect Paul's ministry.

> Brethren, my heart's desire and prayer to God for Israel is, that they might be saved (Rom. 10:1).

Now remember, the above words immediately follow those awesome words in Romans 9. There is no chapter in all of the Word of God that exalts sovereign election like the ninth chapter of Romans. "Therefore hath he mercy on whom he will have mercy, and whom he will he hardeneth" (Romans 9:18), does not sound very 'free-willish' to me. That is high, high, Calvinism. And yet the man who wrote those awesome words immediately says that he longs to see those same people described in chapter nine converted. He sincerely prays for them and continues to witness to them. Human logic may say it is a waste of time, but that did not stop the great apostle from preaching the gospel to all men and pleading with God to open their hearts to believe.

Predestination was the ground upon which Paul appealed to believers when he urged them to worship and praise God.

We have already covered one of the most obvious texts that teach this truth. You might want to look again at the first chapter and review the comments on 2 Thessalonians 2:13. Notice especially that election is the source of joy and thanksgiving. The next text is one my favorite verses in all of Scripture. I will never forget the way God taught me its meaning.

> For who maketh thee to differ from another? and what hast thou that thou didst not receive? now if thou didst receive it, why dost thou glory, as if thou hadst not received it (1 Cor. 4:7)?

In my first pastorate, I had to work part time. One morning before I went to work, I read the fourth chapter of 1 Corinthians. Verse seven jumped out at me and I could not quit thinking about it. On my way to work I picked up an elderly African-American man. He told me some of the horrible things that had happened to him because of the wicked prejudice against the color of his skin. As he talked, I kept thinking, "Who maketh thee to differ from another?" Why did that man suffer all those injustices of which I knew nothing in my life? Why was the color of his skin different from mine?

I have often asked the congregation to look at the color of their hands. Some may be black, others white or red or yellow. However, regardless of the color, the individual's 'free will' had nothing to do with choosing that color. No person is either white or black by his or her own choice. It was God himself who made every Indian red, every Chinese person yellow, every African-American black, and every white man white. Our so-called free wills had nothing to do with our births. The very first sight that any and every person reading these words could have seen was a mother in a loin cloth carrying you off to the Ganges river to throw you in as a sacrifice. None of us said, "If I cannot be born in a middle class home in America, I simply refuse to be born." No! No! "Who maketh thee to differ from another" in the color of your skin or the national and economic conditions of your birth? And, as Paul adds, since it was God alone who made the difference, how dare anyone boast or be prejudiced?

As I pulled into my boss's driveway, I saw his twenty-four-year-old son wearing only a large diaper. He was playing with a little rubber hammer. He had the mentality of a one-year-old. I kept thinking, "Who maketh thee to differ from another?" I had graduated from high school and seminary. I had two healthy children who were doing well in school. Did I, with my "free will," or my children with their "free will," refuse to be born mentally retarded? Did you decide with your "free will," "If I cannot have at least a good enough IQ to graduate from high school, I simply refuse to have anything to do with this thing called life?" No! No! Every person who reads these words could have been born a Down's syndrome child. "Who maketh thee to differ from another" includes not only the color of one's skin but also the capacity of his brain.

I pastored a church were there was a boy with Downs Syndrome in the congregation. We would always hug each other and I would say, "How is my friend David?" He would smile and say, "I am fine. How is my friend John?" One Sunday evening I preached on God's Sovereign Providence. After the customary hug and greeting, I said, "David, I do not know how much you understood of what I said tonight. However, someday all of the Christ rejecters, who were too 'educated' to believe the gospel, will wish they had been like you. They will cry to the rocks to hide them from the face of God and wish they had been born with Down's Syndrome. I do not understand mental illness but I know what I just said will surely happen.

The evening of the day of which I am speaking I stopped at the post office on my way home from work to get my mail. As I put my key into box 221, I heard a guy use my name with a string of curse words. "John Reisinger, you blinkety blank so and so, how are you?" I turned around and saw a man I had not seen for years. We had been in the Navy together, and the last time I had seen him was on Guadalcanal, when we had been drunk all night. He said, "Let's go have a beer and talk over old times." I said, "Ah, well, ah, I don't do that anymore." I then told him the gospel and that I was a preacher. He was silent for several minutes and then burst out laughing and said, "That is the best one you ever told yet." He thought I was putting him on. I had to take him around the corner and show him my name on the bulletin board of the church before he would believe me.

As the man walked away shaking his head, the tears rolled down my cheeks as I thought, "Who maketh thee to differ from another." I think I would have gotten angry if someone would have said to me, "John, the difference between that man and you is this: you were willing to believe but he was not." I knew the difference between us was nothing at all in either him or myself. The difference was in the sovereign electing purposes of God.

My dear Christian brother or sister, I do not care if we are talking about your nationality, or the color of your skin, or your salvation. In every case it was decided by God's sovereign predestination and had nothing to do with your so-called free will. The same thing is true of your physical health and mental ability. Whether you are a genius or a slow learner, you did not choose your IQ with your so-called free will. You must say, "It was God who made me to differ from another." Your personal salvation must be treated the same way. If you are one of Christ's sheep and rejoice in his free forgiveness, it is only because he chose you to be a sheep. Your free will did not enable a goat to change itself into a sheep. It was God's sovereign electing grace that "made you to differ from another."

I trust you can see the point that Paul is making. He is using election to destroy both our arrogant self-sufficiency and our constant tendency to stupid prejudice. No one who understands and feels the truth of 1 Corinthians 4:7 can ever again look down his or her nose at anybody. That person cannot boast, because, as Paul says, "Whatever you have you received is from God alone."

Paul based his appeals to believers to be holy on the fact of their election.

It is no accident that Paul's epistles always begin with doctrine. He does not appeal for a right response until he first gives a clear and convincing reason for demanding that response. In other words, doctrine precedes duty as the essential foundation for the duty. Duty is urged as the only logical response to the doctrine set forth. 1 Corinthians 6:19, 20 is the typical Pauline method of appealing to believers to be holy.

> What? know ye not that… ye are not your own? For ye are bought with a price: *therefore* glorify God in your body, and in your spirit, which are God's (1 Cor. 6:19, 20).

Do you see the force of the argument? The appeal to glorify God in all things is based on a logical and doctrinal *therefore*. Why do I owe God perfect obedience in all that I do? Because I am not my own but belong entirely to him, and I belong to him simply because he bought me with the blood of his Son.

Does the object purchased choose its purchaser, or does the one who pays the price choose what he wants to buy? The purchaser is the one acting and the object being purchased is passive. Did you choose God and ask him to purchase you or did God purchase you because he first chose you to be purchased? How can a believer not want to glorify God? It would be insane for a true child of God not to sincerely want to please the one who purchased him out of sin, shame, guilt, and death! And, I might add, God has given all of his sheep, without a single exception, a "sound mind" (cf. 2 Tim. 1:7)

A careful study of all of Paul's epistles will find this principle to be the norm: first doctrine and then appeal to personal behavior. To say, as many sincere sentimentalists today say, "Never mind doctrine; let's just have practical living," is to miss Paul's message. The message of Paul is this: "It is impossible to have godly practical living without first laying a foundation of sovereign grace where the only possible response can be holy living. Look at two examples.

> I therefore, the prisoner of the Lord, beseech you that ye walk worthy of the vocation wherewith ye are called (Eph. 4:1).

This appeal for a worthy walk is the first such exhortation in the epistle. The first three chapters talk about doctrine. The truth of sovereign election is set forth in chapter one; the depths of depravity out of which we have been raised in regeneration is laid out in chapter two; and the amazing grace of God and its attendant blessings which have been freely given to every believer is explained in chapter three. All of this is through our union with Christ. Ephesians 4:1 is Paul's first use of the word *therefore* in the 'doctrine/response' sense. Paul did use the word *therefore* previously in Ephesians 2:19, but that was not as the basis of an appeal but to establish a point of doctrine. Chapters one through three are pure theology. They show the great blessings a child of God has just because of being joined to Christ. The *therefore* in Ephesians. 4:1 is the same as saying, "Now because everything I said in the three previous chapters is true, the only possible logical and sane response is for you to walk in your daily life in a way that brings glory to the one who lavished all these aforementioned blessings on you."

Paul does the same thing in Romans. Romans Chapters 1 through 11 is doctrine, doctrine, and more doctrine. The first appeal of any kind whatever does not appear until 6:11. The exhortation in Romans 12:1 can only be understood by seeing that "the mercies of God" are referring back to the first eleven chapters.

> I beseech you therefore, brethren, by the mercies of God, that ye present your bodies a living sacrifice, holy, acceptable unto God, which is your reasonable service (Rom. 12:1).

Notice Paul's appeal to reason. It is only reasonable that a child of God should present himself, and all that he is, to God because of God's sovereign electing grace (Rom. 1–11). Anything else is insane and irrational, and I repeat, God has given all of his true saints a 'sane mind.'

Is doctrine important? According to Paul, it is if you want to earnestly appeal to believers to live a holy life. Have you ever noticed that the hymns that glorify God's amazing grace are the ones that inspire you to be "lost in wonder and praise"? The more a hymn exalts God's amazing grace, the more it moves us to want to love and serve our great God and Savior. That is Paul's approach.

Let me quickly say a word about some of the specific effects the doctrine of election should have on us as individuals. It must make us humble and make us grateful for special grace. This was Paul's goal in writing to the Corinthians.

> For ye see your calling, brethren, how that not many wise men after the flesh ... But God hath chosen the foolish things of the world ... God hath chosen the weak things of the world ... That no flesh should glory in his presence.... That, according as it is written, He that glorieth, let him glory in the Lord (1 Cor. 1:26, 27, 29,31).

For just a moment, imagine that you are responsible—because of your free will—for your faith in Christ. You are saved only because you were willing to believe the gospel with your so-called free will. You could not in honesty utter the above words. You would have to say, as some Arminians are quite willing to do, "I, with my *own free will,* am the decisive factor that enabled God to save me. The only reason his eternal plan of salvation worked in my case, and not in another case, is the simple fact that I, with my free will, was willing to repent and believe the gospel." If that is the case, then what specific thing do you owe to God anymore than any other person? Put another way, did God do everything for every lost man that he did for you? If not, then exactly what has God done for you that he did not also do for every lost person in this world?

You may be saying, God loved the whole world just as much as me, *"But I... I alone* made the difference between myself and other people. The difference has nothing at all to do with the electing love of God. It has to do with my free will."

You may be saying, Christ died for every person in this world in the same sense in which he died for me, *"But I...I* took advantage of what Christ equally provided for everyone. I accepted the redemption that was made for me and all other sinners. Christ redeemed all men in the identical same sense that he redeemed me, but I took advantage of it and believed. The only real difference between myself and the man in hell is that *I, with my free will,* enabled the atonement of Christ to be effective and actually save me."

You may be saying, the Holy Spirit convicted others in the same sense and to the same degree that he convicted me, *"But I...I* allowed, with my free will, the Holy Spirit to give me a new heart. I was not, as others, unwilling to cooperate with Holy Spirit in regeneration. I wanted, with my free will, to be born again."

My sincere question is this: Which approach leads to glory in self and the power of free will, and which approach leads to worship and praise of both the grace and the power of the triune God? Does the clear answer to that possibly explain why there is so little genuine amazement and praise in the life and worship of believers today? How can we expect believers to fall flat on their faces in worship and praise to God for any kind of special grace when we constantly tell them, "God has done all he can do; it is now entirely up to you and your free will?" The depth of your gratitude to God will be in direct proportion to the depth of your understanding of what you really owe to him in salvation. The *But I* theology of free will can only have a shallow gratitude because it has a shallow view of debtorship.

My dear reader, *you* may approach the throne of mercy and say, "Sovereign Lord, I am so happy that I decided to give you a chance to save me. I'm so delighted that my free will allowed you to do what you longed to do but could not do until I agreed to allow you to do it." I say, you may speak thus, but as for me and my house, we will sing the following hymn:

> Why was I made to hear thy voice,
> And enter while there's room,
> When thousands make a wretched choice,
> And rather starve than come"?

> 'Twas the same love that spread the feast
> That sweetly drew us in;
> Else we had still refused to taste,
> And perished in our sin

It is an undeniable fact that God chooses some sinners to be saved and leaves others to perish. However, we know that none are chosen because of either their own goodness or their willingness to be chosen. "But," says an objector, "the Bible specifically says that God is not a respecter of persons" (Rom. 2:11). If God, as an objector will assert, looked down through history and saw that some sinners would be willing to be chosen then God could say, "I have found some sinners with a willing heart and I now have a basis upon which to choose them to be saved." In such a scenario, God is a respecter of man's foreseen faith. Such a view truly makes God a respecter of persons.

Romans 2:11 does not mean that God cannot or does not show grace to only some men but not all men, since the Bible clearly teaches that He does that very thing. It means that there is nothing about any man's person or personage, especially foreseen faith, which makes him different in God's sight from any other sinner. There is nothing that any man has ever done or will do that God can respect and reward. Therefore when God chooses a particular sinner to be saved, it must be purely on the basis of sovereign grace and not foreseen faith.

I cannot emphasize strongly enough what we said in the first chapter. There is both a sovereign election of *some* unto salvation, and there is a sincere and universal proclamation of the gospel to *all* men without exception or distinction (cf. John 6:37 and Matt. 11:20–28).

Ah, my dear reader, may I say a pointed word to you? If you perish in hell, your lips will never accuse God of being unjust or unfair. You will never blame God's election for your eternal destruction. If you have read this booklet this far, or if you have been in meetings where I have preached, then you have heard the gospel. You have been urged to trust Christ. If you refuse to repent and believe the gospel, you will perish with that gospel in your ears. You will plead guilty and will never even think of accusing the most high God or his sovereign electing grace as the reason you are in hell.

However, just the opposite is true of the saint who makes it to heaven. In that land of glory, no one will even know how to spell the words *free will*. No saint will talk about "giving God a chance" or "allowing God to save him or her." All boasting in the free will of man will be left behind. Let the saints come down from heaven and testify and their theme will be sovereign grace. They will, without exception cry, "Salvation is of the Lord, from beginning to end."

Imagine you are a four-legged sheep caught in a thicket from which you cannot free yourself. You are cold, hungry, thirsty, and your throat is sore from bleating. The more you struggle to get free, the more the briars dig into your flesh and cause the blood to flow. Finally, in utter despair, you resign yourself to your pitiful situation, quit struggling, and prepare to die. If, in that most hopeless situation, you heard the familiar voice of a shepherd calling your name, what would you do? You would cry, "Baaaa! Baaaa!" as loudly as you could.

Well, let me tell you that if you are a two-legged sheep in the same condition, you will react exactly the same way. If you are caught in a thicket of sin and cannot get lose, and the harder you try to get free the more you fail because the bonds of sin get stronger, and you are hungry, tired, and thirsty, then I have *good news*. There is a gracious Shepherd calling your name. Cry out to him. Cry, "Baaaa! Baaaa!" as loudly as you can. Tell him how sick you are of sin and its awful consequences. Tell him how totally helpless you are and how desperately you need his grace and power. He will be at your side in a moment. He will free you from the thicket of sin, bind up your wounds, give you bread and water, and put you on his shoulder and carry you safely back to the fold.

The only person who will not cry out "Baaa! Baaa!" is the person who either does not believe he is caught in a thicket of sin, but imagines he is totally free, or the person who loves the sin despite the misery it brings.

If you are a chosen sheep, you know what it is to be set free from the thicket. You have tasted the Bread of Heaven and have drunk the Water of Life. You will praise forever him who loved you with an everlasting love and washed you in his own precious blood.